HH ARCHITECTS
ARCHITECTURAL DESIGN OFFICE | HYEYOUNG HAN

MASS-K
ARCHITECTURE IMAGEWORKS STUDIO | WONSEOK LEE

BRIQUE

Butterfly House

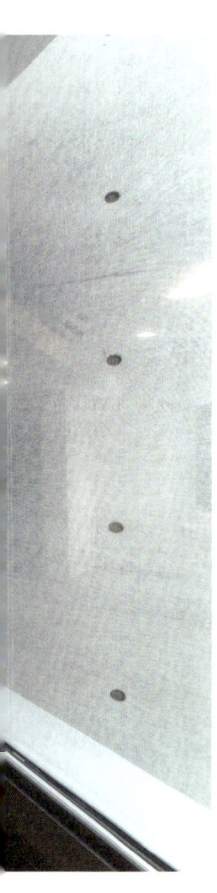

54 / 55

Despite its unique exterior,

the Butterfly House

is highly functional
and lives up to all expectations
for a comfortable suburban house.

At first glance, the Butterfly House might seem like the kind of expensive home a stuck-up art gallery director would live in. In some ways, it projects notions of uber-planned architectural design. The angular shapes, monotone colors, elaborately calculated exteriors, and eccentric interior space all add to the house's uniqueness. Yet, despite these avant-garde elements, the homeowners are an ordinary couple with two kids.

The husband commutes to work not far from the house. On weekends, he creates and builds in his home workshop. He has repurposed steel pipes and stair boards from construction materials into benches, and has installed a climbing wall for the kids on the retaining wall in the backyard. The workshop on the mezzanine below the stairs and the 5m-high garage suit his handyman needs.

The wife shared with BRIQUE her happy moments raising the kids in a detached house. When everyone leaves for work or school, she strolls around the yard. Walking past the sandbox in the front yard, and turning the corner of the house along the yard with pebbles, there is a backyard that is completely hidden from the outside. By day this space is a playground where the kids can play basketball and wall climb. At night it is an outdoor cafe' where the couple can talk over a beer. Around the corner to the front yard, there is a swimming pool with a view of the mountain. The wife sits in the kitchen, savoring the best view in the house with a cup of tea before starting her day.

To the family's delightfully active children, the whole house is a playground. If they get too hot playing in the sandbox, they take a quick dip in the pool. On a cool evening, they play ball on the grassy lawn. The house offers plenty of hiding spots that are revealed only from the upstairs view. It is a home designed to stimulate a child's imagination.

The architect considers herself lucky to have met clients willing to eschew the prejudice that a room must always be square. The clients understood the advantages of a triangle-shaped room and were excited about the new space. They were also convinced that a pool was essential for everybody. The architect decided to introduce pointy shapes into the design in order to satisfy legal limitations while enhancing the lighting and view. She also strived to create functional lines. The opus created from these concepts was the Butterfly House, which provides visual openness and originality.

However, the house is not yet perfect. A house's mission is fulfilled only when it is continuously renewed from being filled with a cycle of new people. The Butterfly House is still in this process of completion.

_ Hyeyoung Han

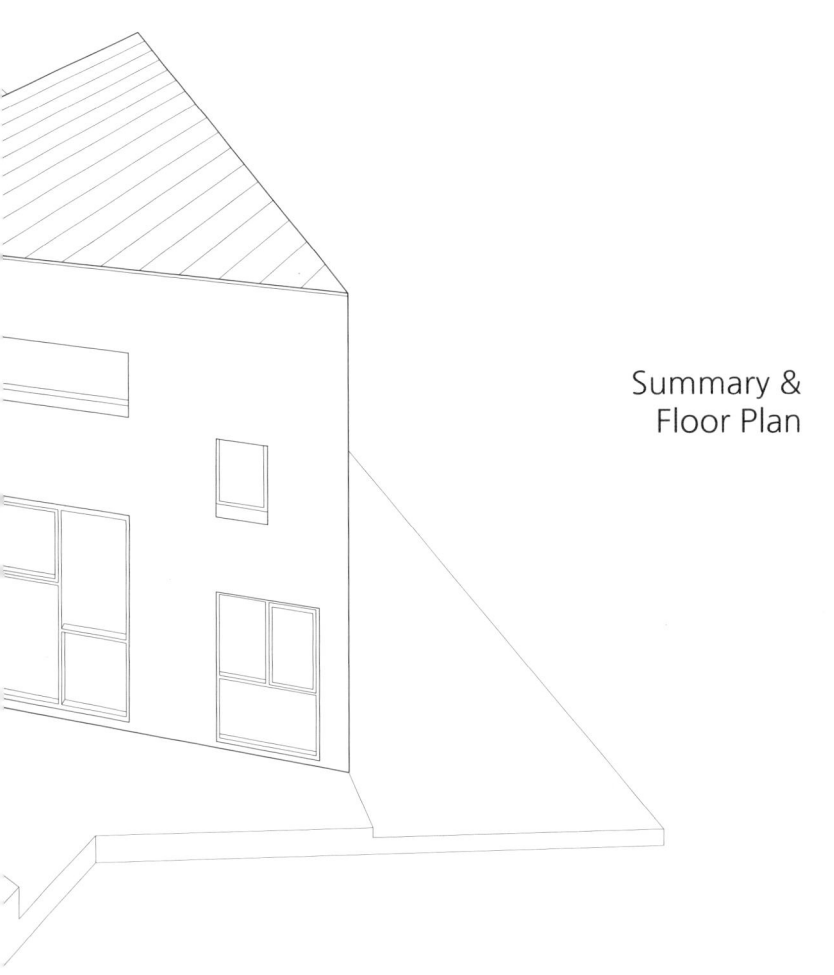

Summary &
Floor Plan

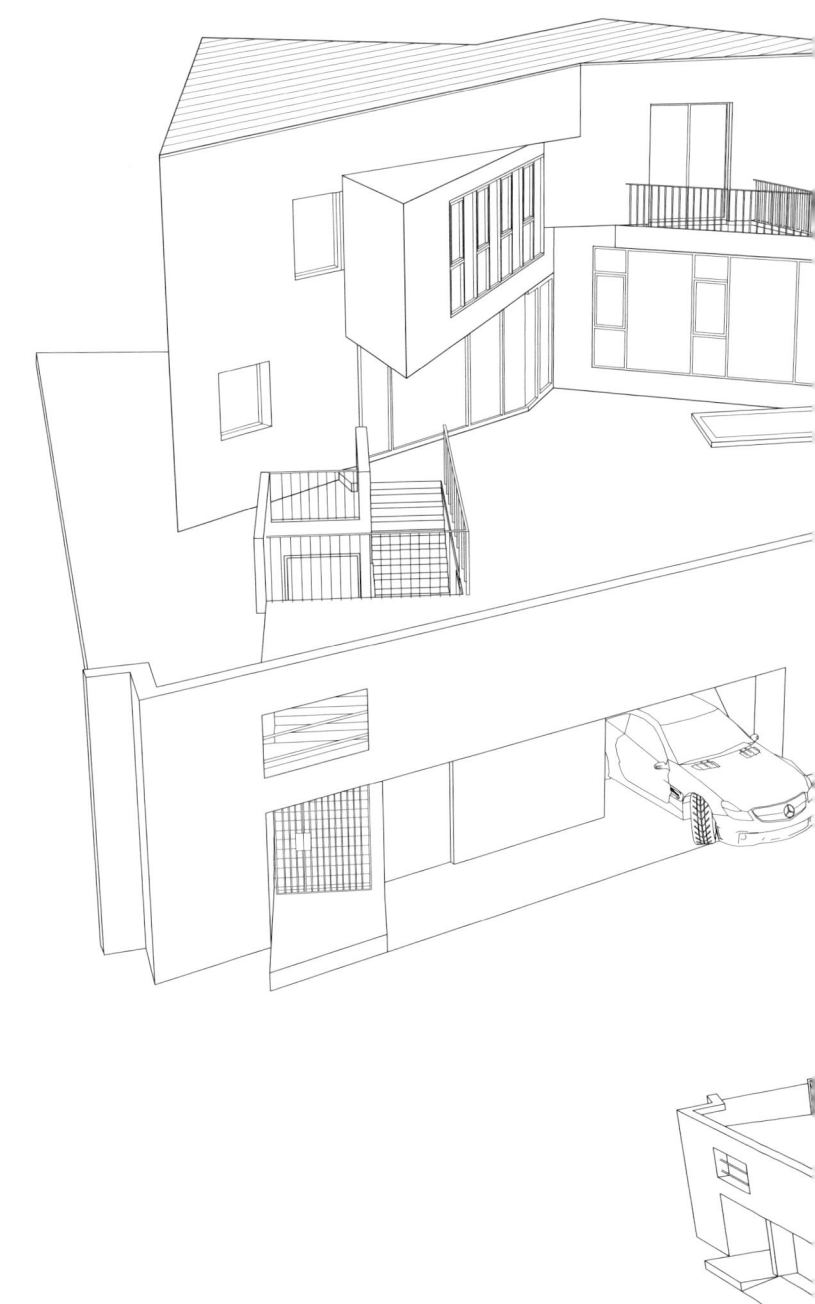

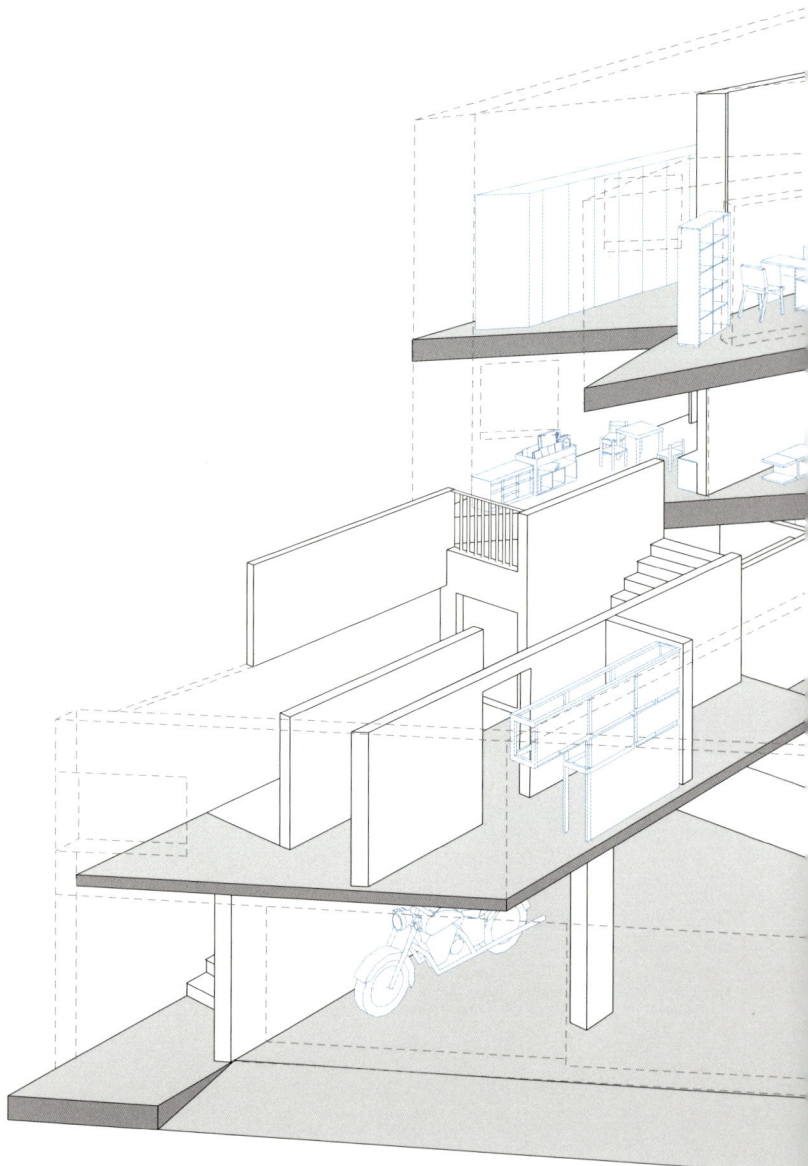

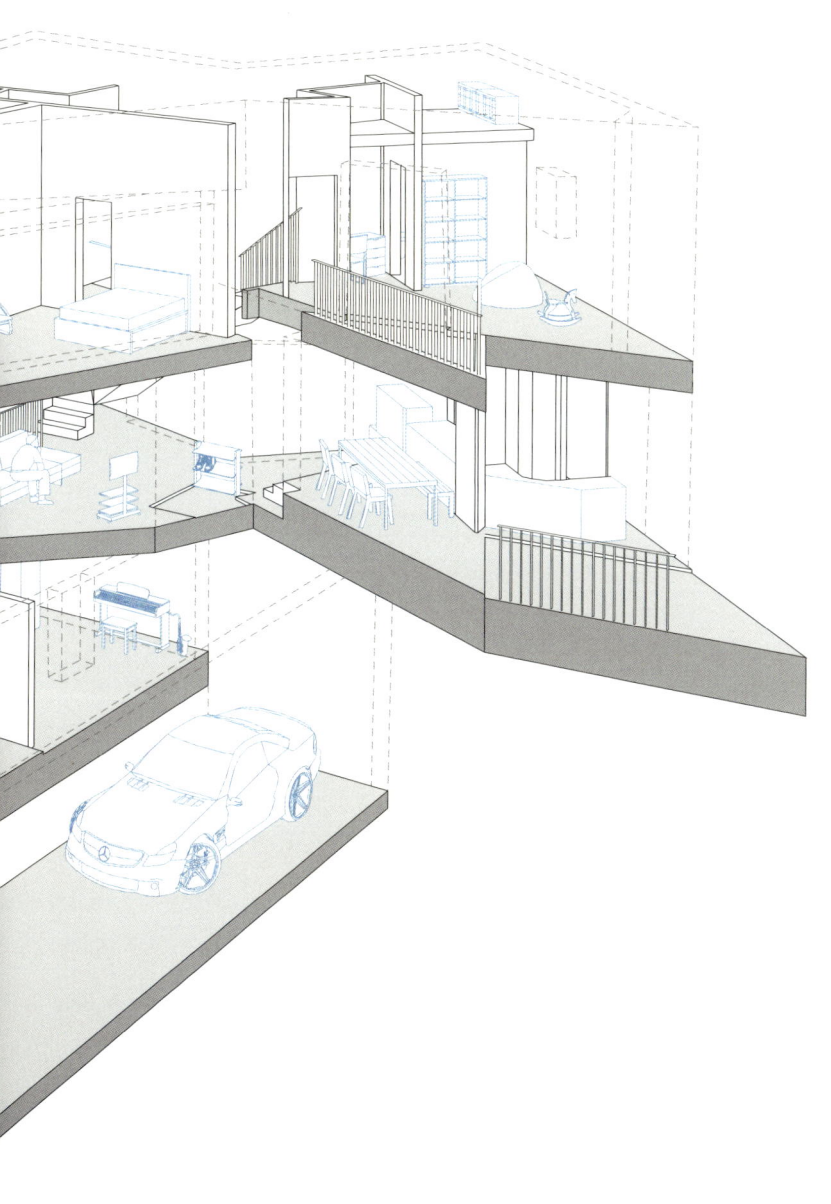

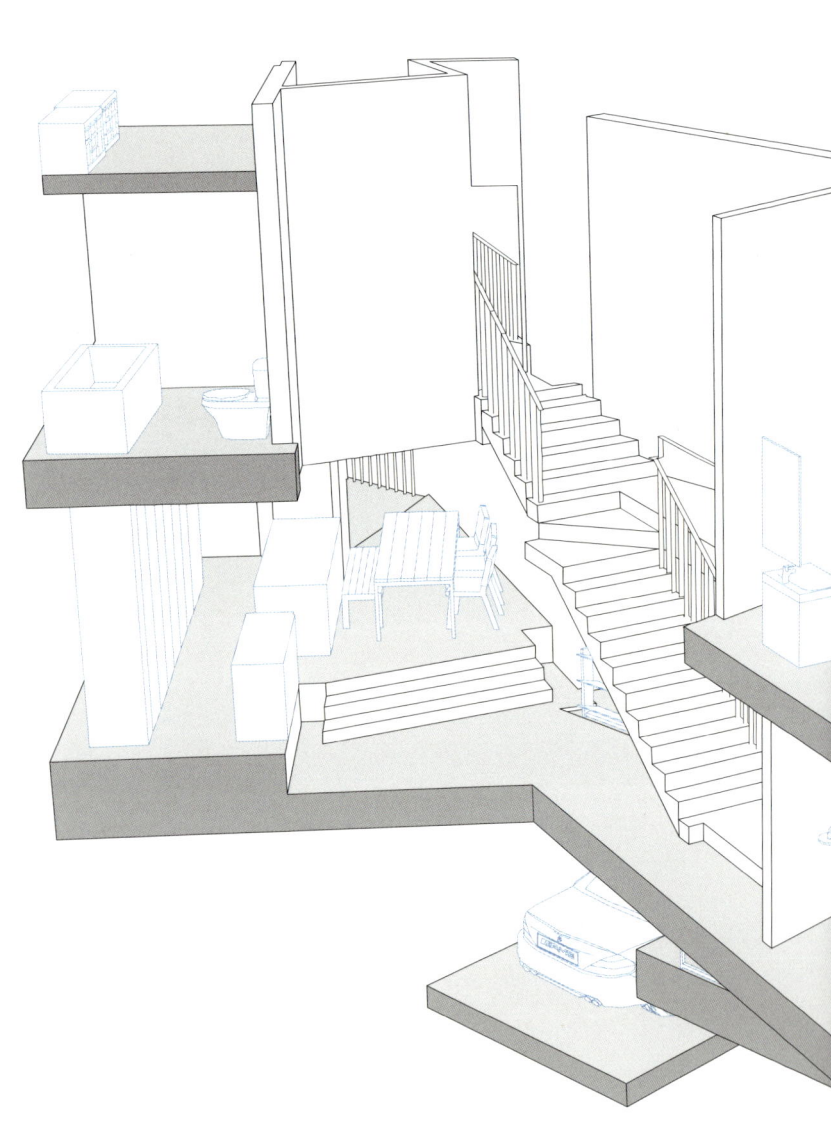

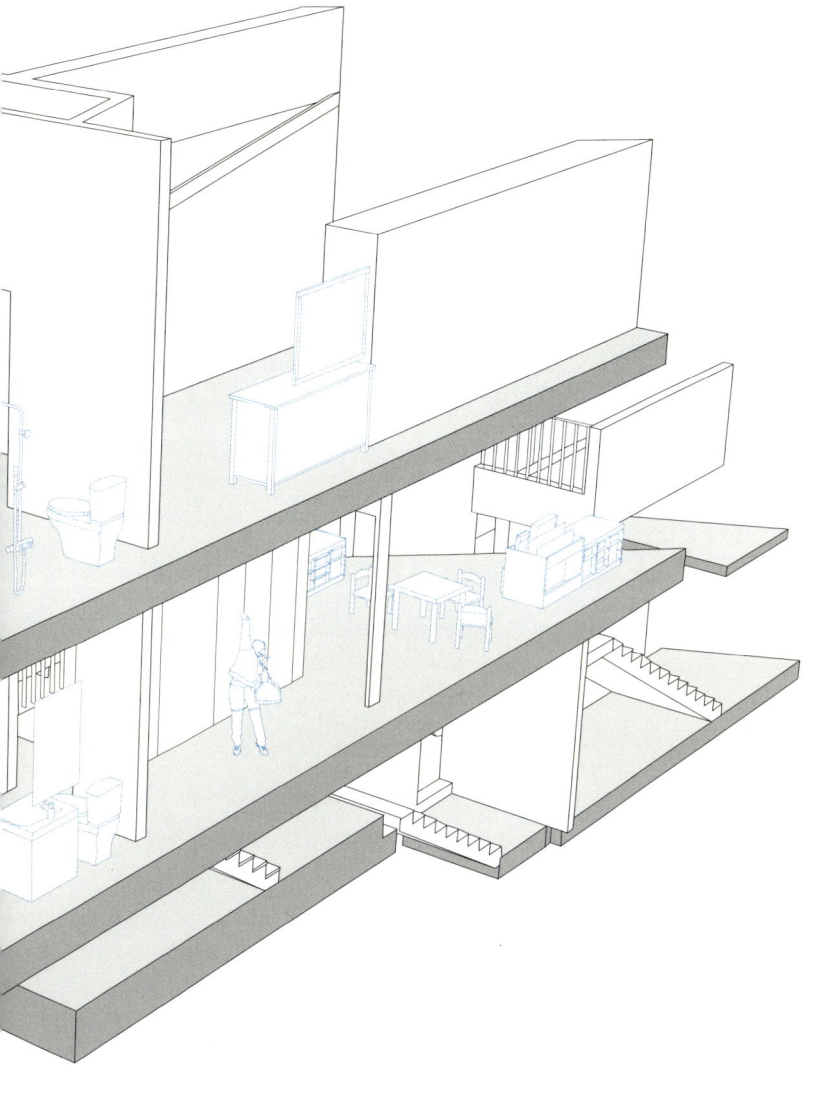

⌖ 1st FLOOR PLAN

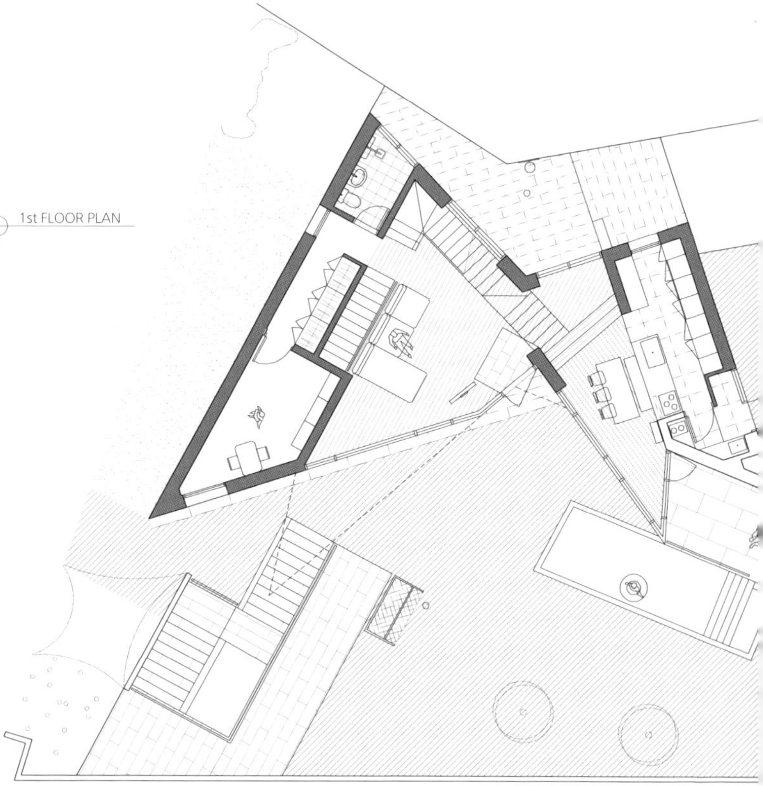

⌖ -1st FLOOR PLAN

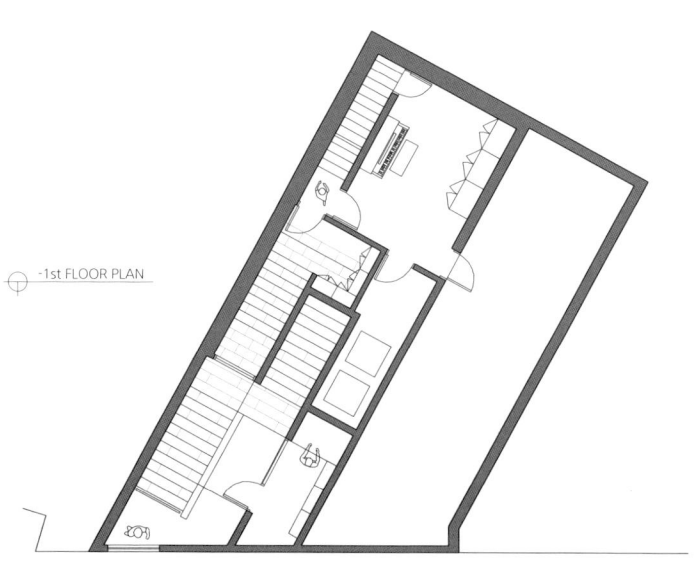

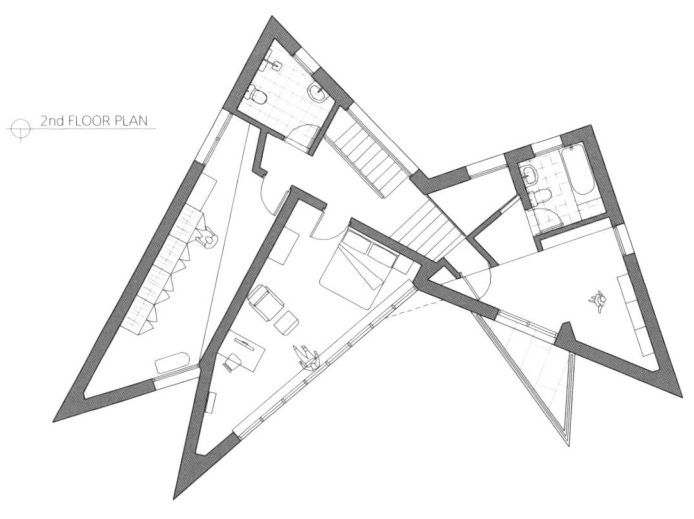

2nd FLOOR PLAN

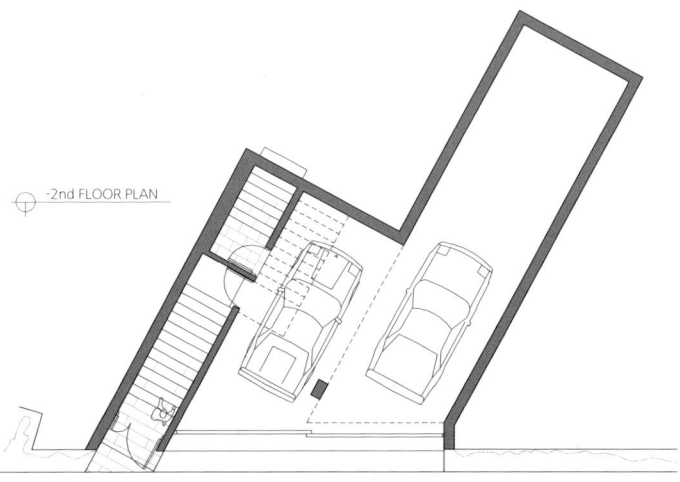

-2nd FLOOR PLAN

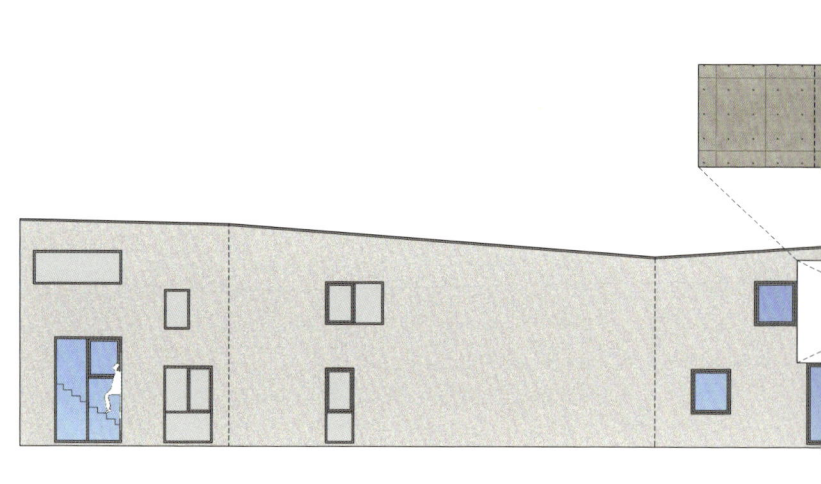

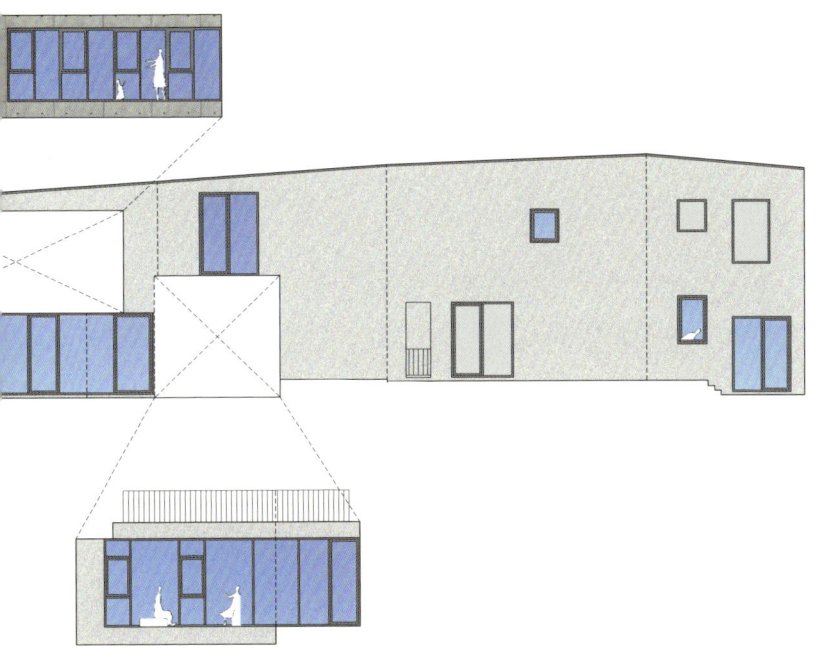

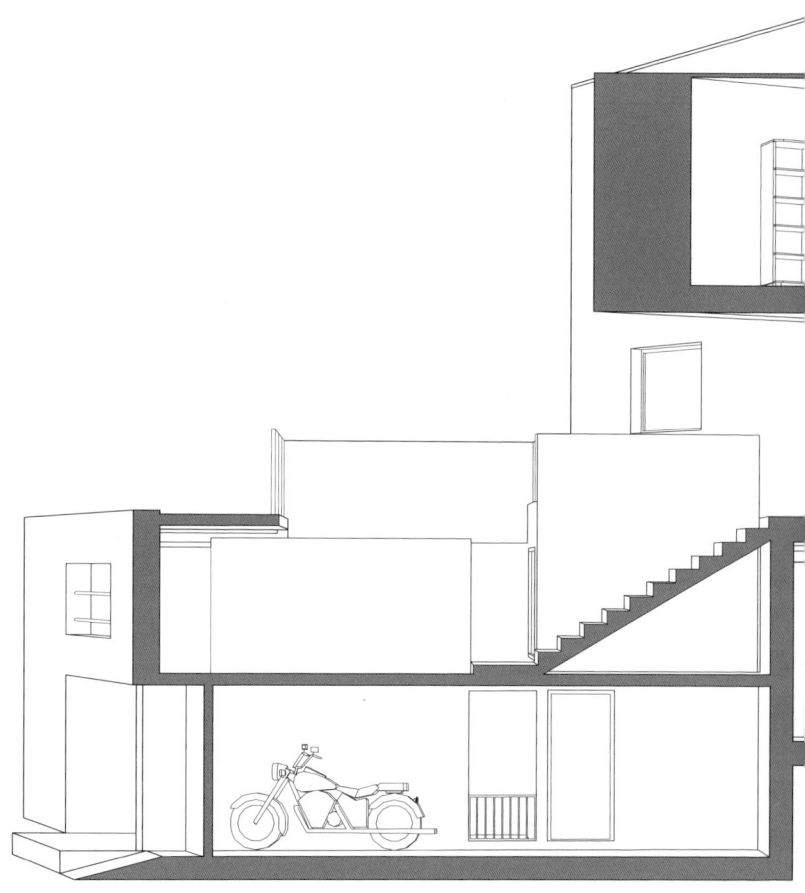

+ Location: Nam-dong, Cheonin-gu, Yongin-si, Korea
+ Site Area: 448.00m²
+ Gross Floor Area: 89.18m²
+ Total Floor Area: 268.01m²
+ Building Coverage Ratio: 19.90%
+ Floor Area Ratio: 36.22%
+ Building Scope: 2 above ground and 2 underground stories
+ Design Period: 2015.08-2016.02
+ Construction Period: 2016.03-2016.10

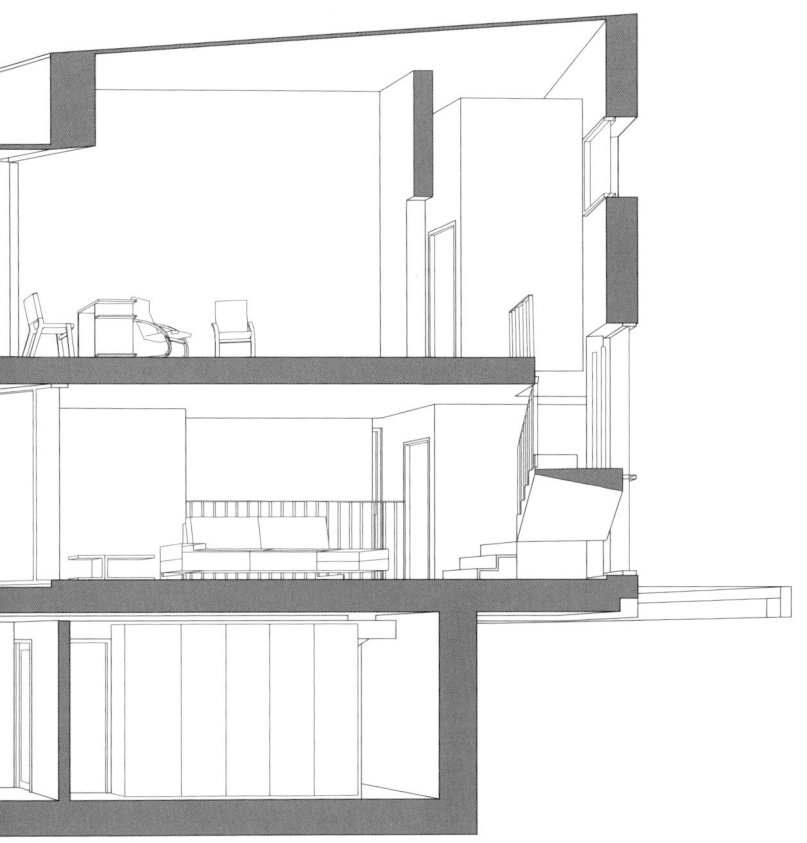

_Architect: Hyeyoung Han·HH Architects/ Architectural Design Office
_Staff: Soomin Lee, Shinhye Kim
_Construction: Seers Design Group
_Drawing: Hyeyoung Han, Soomin Lee
_Client: Boyoung Choi

Photography
WONSEOK LEE

MASS-K | Architecture Imageworks Studio
274, Nonhyeon-dong, Gangnam-gu, Seoul, KOREA
kariyas@gmail.com
www.mass-k.com

> **An architecture photographer who reconfigures ordinary spaces into unique aesthetic spaces**

Photographer Wonseok Lee transcends the boundaries of architectural photography and religious art. His interests lie in the spiritual spaces created by the organic balance between form and sanctity.

Lee holds an MA in photography from Hongik University, and now teaches media art at the university level. He is a representative of Studio Mass-K and a collaborating photographer at Sony. In 2015, he became the first Korean to receive the SEGD Award. His works include DDP (Seoul, 2015) and Sarang Church (Seoul, 2014).

Architect
HYEYOUNG HAN

HH Architects | Architectural Design Office
21-10, Jinkwan 1-ro, Eunpyeong-gu, Seoul, Korea
hh_architects@hotmail.com
www.hharchitects.co.kr

> **An architect fascinated by all things small, old, and peripheral**

Architect Hyeyoung Han is curious about smaller, older, and non-centralized things. It is her philosophy in her architectural, interior design, and furniture design projects that very trivial things in the environment add up to form everyday life. She has worked at One O One Architects, Iarc Architects, and OCA Architects on various projects with diverse styles and colors. She holds a BA in Architecture from Kookmin University and an MA in Architectural Engineering from the Graduate School of Engineering at the Universidad Politecnica de Madrid, Spain. She is currently teaching at Kookmin University and Wonkwang University.

Her major projects include serving as the consulting manager of the "Creating Happy Cultural Spaces" initiative organized by the KCDF in 2015, and working as the architect for the "local bookstore in Gyeonggi" project in 2017. She was the architect for the Two Houses in Seongbuk-dong (2017), the Butterfly House in Nam-dong (2016) and Multicultural Family Project in Gunpo (2016).

BRIQUE DESIGN BOOK vol.2_**BUTTERFLY HOUSE**

Published in Korea in 2018 by BRIQUE Company
www.brique.co; info@brique.co
ISBN 979-11-960430-5-6 / 979-11-960430-0-1(set)
Authors: Hyeyoung Han, Wonseok Lee
Edited and designed by Soyeon Lee
Translated by Hawon Yoo, Ksan Rubadeau
All rights reserved ⓒ 2018 BRIQUE, and the individual contributors

* 이 도서의 국립중앙도서관 출판예정도서목록(CIP)은 서지정보유통지원시스템 홈페이지(http://seoji.nl.go.kr)와
국가자료공동목록시스템(http://www.nl.go.kr/kolisnet)에서 이용하실 수 있습니다. (CIP제어번호 : CIP2018010152)

Inspiring Architecture & Interior Concepts
BRIQUE DESIGN BOOK

II

KRW 15,600
04610

ISBN 979-11-960430-5-6
ISBN 979-11-960430-0-1 (SET)

www.brique.co
All images are © each office/photographer mentioned.